Original title:
Rhyme of the Rainfall

Copyright © 2025 Creative Arts Management OÜ
All rights reserved.

Author: Cameron Blair
ISBN HARDBACK: 978-1-80567-359-0
ISBN PAPERBACK: 978-1-80567-658-4

Harmonies in the Hail

A tap dance on the window pane,
Tiny ice cubes, what a gain!
Sipping tea and snoring loud,
As the sky wears a fluffy cloud.

Puddles jump like eager frogs,
Dancing with their soggy logs.
The dogs parade in rain slickers,
Chasing drops like happy flickers.

Ballad of the Bursting Sky

Oh look, the clouds are having a feast,
Dropping goodness, at least not least!
Umbrellas fly like kites on the run,
While puddles deep in splashes have fun.

Kids run wild with laughter in tow,
Splashing muddy pies, oh what a show!
The sun sneaks out for a quick peek,
Winking at the chaos, just a little cheek!

Sonnet of the Silver Streams

Glistening streams that trickle and giggle,
A prankster's playground, time to wiggle!
Socks on hands and hats on toes,
This silly dance is how it goes.

The lawn's a canvas for tiny feet,
With every splash, a laughter beat.
Flowers sigh as raindrops fall,
Joined in this hilarious brawl.

Couplet of the Cloudburst

Clouds let loose with boisterous cheer,
Raining laughter that all can hear.
The cat in boots takes a soggy stroll,
While squishy green frogs aim for the goal.

Heavy coats and silly hats,
Floating down the street like frumpy brats.
Under splashy skies, joy rebounds,
Chasing rainbows that know no bounds!

Stanzas in the Shimmering Showers

Puddles dance like tiny feet,
Raindrops tap a silly beat.
Umbrellas flip in gusty glee,
While ducks quack, 'Come splash with me!'

Clouds wear hats that look so bright,
Sprinkling joy, a funny sight.
We slip and slide, turn round and round,
In this wet and wacky ground.

Odes to the Overcast

The sky is gray, the mood is light,
Rainy days bring pure delight.
Socks are soggy, yet we grin,
As puddles beckon us to spin.

Rubber ducks in streams do sail,
Waving to the weatherman's tale.
Lightning flashes, we jump and squeal,
Oh, what fun to dance and heal!

Cadence of the Cascades

Waterfall giggles, a cheerful laugh,
Splishing and splashing, a wet giraffe.
It tickles toes, it splatters clothes,
With every step, a story grows.

Raindrops plop on a bearded tree,
Sharing jokes with bumblebees.
Nature laughs, while we all gleam,
Making memories, like a dream.

Tapestry of Tumbling Waters

Down the street, the rivers flow,
With rogue leaves in a bright show.
Laughter echoes, a splashy grin,
As we race the wind to win.

Puddles join in a singing spree,
While gophers hide, but peek with glee.
Rainy days bring forth surprises,
With every drop, joy is now rising.

Cascading Cadences of Calm

Pitter-patter on the ground,
A tap dance from the clouds around.
Umbrellas flip, hats go fly,
As puddles form, we laugh and sigh.

The ducks quack loud, they're quite the sight,
Waddling through the water with delight.
Children splash in every pool,
Rainy days, oh, how cool!

Melodies of the Moisture

Drip-drop, a tune is played,
On rooftops where the raindrops weighed.
Singing leaves, they dance and sway,
While soggy socks are on display.

The air gets fresh, the breeze a tease,
So I'll wear my galoshes with ease.
And as the rain begins to pour,
I'll prance about and beg for more!

Splotches and Stanzas on the Soil

Mud pies made with glee abound,
Cakes for critters in the ground.
Worms wiggle in a merry line,
While I trip over roots, oh how divine!

Each drop a laugh, a silly joke,
A splash of fun with every poke.
Nature's party, sticky and bright,
In this muddy mess, I feel just right!

Variations of the Vaporous Veil

Look up high, see clouds collide,
Creating portraits of joy worldwide.
They roll and tumble, what a show,
As rainbows peek through, the colors glow.

With every splash and every grin,
Friends come over, let the games begin!
We'll race the raindrops, one, two, three,
Life's a dance, come splash with me!

Whirlwinds and Whispers in Water

Puddles giggle, splashes play,
As umbrellas dance their wobbly sway.
Raindrops tap a silly tune,
While frogs croak jokes beneath the moon.

Winds swirl round like a wild kite,
Chasing clouds, oh what a sight!
Each drop sings its own refrain,
In squishy boots, we jump again.

Squirrels skitter, zoom and sway,
While fat raindrops block the way.
With rubber ducks we float and twirl,
In river streams, our laughter swirls.

So let it pour, let breezes tease,
In puddle pools, we dance with ease.
Each splash a chuckle, what a blast!
Oh, bring on the wet and wild forecast!

The Elegance of Every Exhalation

Clouds puff up like cotton candy,
While raindrops land, so sweet and dandy.
Each drip a note from nature's choir,
As giggles bubble, we never tire.

Waltzing through the puddles bright,
Splashing colors, oh what a sight!
With umbrellas spun like twirling tops,
We stomp our feet, and laughter hops.

Silly hats, they flip and sway,
As rain begins to play its play.
Each droplet dances, skips and prances,
In joyous rhythm, the world enhances.

So sip your tea while raindrops roll,
Giggles echo from every soul.
Embrace the whimsy, let it flow,
In each exhale, let joy grow!

Inflections in the Interludes

Raindrops tap on window panes,
Playing jokes, like silly trains.
Each little trickle, a playful shout,
As puddles call us all about.

With squelchy shoes, we prance and play,
Inevery splash, the world's a ballet.
Frogs in tuxedos jump in style,
As laughter dances for a while.

Each gutter sings a giddy song,
To the rhythm where we belong.
When clouds burst forth in feathered cheer,
We twirl, we leap, we have no fear.

So let the droplets make us giggle,
As we chase the rain in a silly wiggle.
With each soft patter, joy prevails,
In rainfall's dance, our laughter sails!

Melodic Mist and Memory

Pitter patter on my head,
Makes me dance, forget my dread.
A splash of fun in every drop,
I might just slip, but I won't stop.

Silly hats are quite the style,
Umbrellas turn to laughter's smile.
In puddles, we find our best friend,
Jumping high, we never bend.

Each squishy step, a giggle burst,
In this wet world, we're quite immersed.
With raindrops chorusing along,
Who knew that wet could feel so strong?

Memory's fog from this wet haze,
A day of fun that surely stays.
From drips and laughs, our joy begins,
Rainy days, where silliness wins!

The Soundtrack of the Shower

As droplets dance upon the roof,
It's like they're sharing silly proof.
Each splash a note, so soft and sweet,
Conducting chaos under my feet.

Rubber ducks in every lane,
Sing along with the falling rain.
Cups and saucers start to hum,
We create a band with a drum.

The tap's a solo, splashes cheer,
A jazzy vibe I want to hear.
So grab your socks, let's make a band,
In this wet world, we take our stand.

The rhythm keeps the spirits high,
We shake our boots and wave goodbye.
With every beat, our spirits soar,
Turning showers to encore galore!

Vignettes in the Veil of Rain

Raindrops fall like tasty sweets,
Each one a game, a looped retreat.
Splashing laughter fills the air,
Wet feet dance without a care.

Mice in boots hop right along,
Singing out our silly song.
Look at that cat, she's on a spree,
Chasing raindrops with such glee!

Every puddle, a canvas bright,
We draw our dreams with pure delight.
Worms do waltz beneath the ground,
In this watery show, joy is found.

So let the misty moments play,
In this quilted world of gray.
With giggles flowing, hearts do swell,
These rainy tales we know so well!

Sonnet Under the Soaked Trees

Under branched canopies we sway,
In the shower's embrace, we laugh and play.
Soggy shoes and giggly squeaks,
Nature's tickle, cheek to cheeks.

The clouds above, they tease and jest,
With raindrops drumming, we feel so blessed.
From drop to drop, our spirits lift,
In the laughter's warmth, we find a gift.

When raindrops dance on leafy roofs,
A symphony, in our silly hooves.
From every splash, giggles arise,
With puddles reflecting our merry eyes.

So let the storm come, we'll stay bright,
In this soaked world, we find delight.
Each falling drop, a funny face,
In the trees' shade, we find our place!

Lyrical Landscapes in Liquid Light

Raindrops dance on rooftops high,
Splashes giggle, oh my, oh my!
Puddles form like little lakes,
With each joke, the ground just shakes.

Umbrellas flip, a silly sight,
Dancing in the gloom, what a delight!
Cats in boots, splashing around,
Creating joy without a sound.

Notations from the Nimbus Night

Clouds above start to parade,
Making music, a rainy serenade.
Drip-drop, puddles sing in glee,
As lightning flashes jocularly.

Silly hats on people's heads,
Dancing raindrops on their beds!
Jokes are told by every flake,
Each one full of fun to make.

The Tapestry of Teardrops

From the heavens, laughter falls,
Slips and slides down city walls.
Each raindrop tells a funny tale,
Of frogs that jump and snail on scale.

Bicycles splash through their parade,
While I sit safe, a sneaky shade.
With every plop on ground so near,
The world giggles, spreading cheer.

Flowing Forms of the Fluid

A tap-tap-tap upon the glass,
Nature's jesters with each pass.
They bubble, they chuckle, a fun-filled spree,
Making the sober sky dance with glee.

Rain sliding down like slippery soap,
Creating costumes, making us cope.
Laughter echoes from each small pool,
Mud pies await, it's all so cool!

Verses in the Drizzle

Puddles dance beneath my feet,
As raindrops tap a silly beat.
Umbrellas twist like fancy hats,
While ducks parade in soggy flats.

A cat leaps from a window wide,
And finds a splash - it takes a ride!
With every drip the laughter grows,
Complaints drowned out by thunder's prose.

Slippery slides on sidewalks gleam,
I take a tumble, lost in dream.
The droplets grin in gleeful play,
As I roll in the mud today!

Each raindrop has a joke to share,
While raincoats flap with comic flair.
So let's embrace this drizzly spree,
For laughter's best when we're all free!

Symphony of the Soaked Earth

Bubbles bounce in every lane,
As droplets drum their own refrain.
My socks squelch like a concert's jam,
With every step I'm like a lamb.

The wind calls out, 'You'll need a float!'
Suggesting waves in my old coat.
With squishy shoes upon my toes,
I waddle like a duck, who knows?

Dancing vermin, drenched and bold,
Chasing worms in skies of gold.
Each splash and squirt is pure delight,
As clouds unleash their giggling might.

A scene unfolds that's full of glee,
As rainbirds sing and feign a spree.
Let's stomp away all thoughts of gloom,
For wetness blooms in joy's own room!

Lullabies of Liquid Light

Tiny splatters start to play,
They tap-dance here and sway away.
A gutter sings a silly song,
While frogs croak along like they belong.

Clouds in puffs like cotton candy,
Paint the sky in colors dandy.
With every plop, a chuckle grows,
As rain is paired with tickling toes.

Giggling droplets in a race,
Slide down noses, leave a trace.
The world becomes a jolly mess,
With every splash, no time to stress!

So gather 'round, let laughter glide,
In puddles deep, we'll take a ride.
For liquid light brings joy so bright,
In this wild, wet and funny night!

Chants of the Cascading Drops

Pitter patter, what a show!
Nature's band is on the go.
With watery notes that slip and glide,
As giggling gusts cannot abide.

Squirrels skitter, drenched in flair,
Chase each drop through tangled hair.
Raindrops tickle branches high,
While drumming on the roof they sigh.

Colorful boots begin to sink,
As puddles form; it's time to think.
Why not join in the playful sound,
And twirl in joy, merrily found?

Each cascading drop's a chance to play,
In this drenched dreamland, come what may.
With laughter's echo, hearts now soar,
For rainy days are fun galore!

Harmonies of the Heavens

Raindrops fall, a cheerful beat,
They tap-dance on the window seat.
A cat jumps high, then lands with thud,
She thinks the sky has turned to mud.

Umbrellas spin like flying saucers,
While folks splash through like laughing horses.
A puddle's splash, a hearty cheer,
Nature's jest, the rain draws near.

Clouds play peek-a-boo with the sun,
In this parade, there's endless fun.
So grab your boots, come join the play,
In this wet world, we'll dance away.

So let it pour! We'll sing along,
With puddles deep and joy so strong.
Each drop a note in this grand spree,
In this drenched world, we're wild and free.

Pattering Poems in Puddles

Puddles giggle as we leap,
They splash our shoes, oh what a heap!
A dog takes part, he shakes his head,
To him, these drops taste like his bed.

Jump over here, leap over there,
With squishy shoes and soggy hair.
The world is wet, but spirits high,
Let's make some noise, just you and I.

Muddy footprints mark our way,
As rainy clouds begin to play.
A slick wet slide awaits the bold,
A slippery tale soon to be told!

So let it rain, let laughter flow,
Each splash a smile, let good times grow.
In puddles deep, let fun ignite,
Together, we'll dance through the night.

Ballad of the Blustering Breeze

The wind sings loud a merry song,
It flutters leaves, it twirls along.
A gust knocks off an old man's hat,
He chases it like a sneaky cat.

Whistling through the branches tall,
The breeze brings whispers, a playful call.
"Catch me if you can!" it seems to say,
While kites take flight and float away.

A paper boat sails on the stream,
Chased by breezes, it has a dream.
With every gust, it spins and sways,
A little sailor lost in plays.

So let us dance with gales so free,
Join the symphony, just you and me.
With breezes blustering around our feet,
In this wild storm, oh what a treat!

Syllables of the Soaked Earth

The earth hums softly, full of cheer,
As drizzles sound like whispers dear.
With every drop, it giggles bright,
A soggy world, a pure delight.

Mud pies form in nature's bowl,
With splat! splat! splashes, joy's the goal.
Children laugh, they jump and run,
Creating chaos, oh what fun!

Worms wiggle up to see the light,
While flowers sway in pure delight.
This wet embrace, a merry trend,
With every puddle, joy extends.

So let the storm unleash its song,
In this soaked theater, we belong.
With each wet syllable, joy will sprout,
A soggy tale, we'll laugh about!

Lyric of the Lashing Waters

Pitter-patter on my roof,
A tiny tap dance, quite aloof.
Each drop a jester, full of glee,
Splashing puddles, wild and free.

Umbrellas bloom like flowers bright,
In every color, what a sight!
A raincoat dance, it looks absurd,
Who knew the rain could be this weird?

Socks are soggy, squishy shoes,
I slip and slide, what can I lose?
A rubber duck goes racing by,
My laughter echoes, oh my, oh my!

So let it rain, let laughter flow,
With every drop, our spirits grow.
In this wet circus, we'll take a chance,
Grab a friend and join the dance!

Stanzas of the Swirling Storm

Thunder grumbles like a cat,
Raindrops dance on my old hat.
Lightning plays a game of tag,
Under the storm, I do a wag.

Puddles grew, a small lake found,
A boat made of paper sails around.
With rubber boots, I'm quite the sight,
Row by row, I avoid a fright.

Drifting leaves like boats at sea,
They wiggle and giggle just like me.
The wind whispers jokes in my ear,
As I dance, the neighbors cheer!

Stormy weather, what a show!
Splash and laugh as we all go.
With every joke, the skies turn bright,
Who could guess rain brings such delight?

Rhythms from the Raindrops

Tap-tap-tap, the song it sings,
A chorus made of puddle springs.
Hats go flying, hair gets wet,
Oh, the fun, we won't forget!

Clouds are grumpy, wearing frowns,
Yet here we are, in silly gowns.
Water balloons from heaven fall,
A chance to giggle, what a brawl!

Silly ducks in puddles play,
Slipping, sliding, making hay.
Between the splashes, laughter peeks,
A comedy show in rain-soaked streets!

When the sun returns to shine,
We'll recall storms as so divine.
In every drop, a joy unplanned,
We'll dance again, hand in hand!

Haikus of Hidden Dew

Raindrops tickle grass,
Nature laughs under grey skies,
Every drop a tease.

Silly flowers sway,
Dancing in the puddles' gleam,
Chaotic ballet.

A bird takes a dive,
With splashes that make us smile,
Rainy giggles thrive.

Morning dew drops fall,
Like tiny jewels on leaves' tips,
Nature's laughter glows.

Trickle Tunes of Tranquility

Raindrops dance on window panes,
Like timing beats of tiny trains.
Puddles splash with silly cheer,
While ducks in boots waddle near.

Clouds wear hats and silly grins,
As all the raindrops play their spins.
Singing songs of splish-splash fun,
Chasing giggles from everyone.

Droplets twirl like ballerinas,
In wellingtons, not just hyenas.
They leap and twist with carefree grace,
Creating laughter in every place.

So gather round for misty mirth,
As laughter leaps above the earth.
Let the watery concert roll,
With bubbly joy that fills the soul.

The Symphony of the Sullen Skies

When grayish clouds start to convene,
I swear I hear a trumpeting scene.
A flurry of giggles, a grand parade,
As drops measure beats that never fade.

The soggy socks are not so chic,
But watch them dance, oh what a leak!
While lightning cracks a cheeky joke,
Puddles burst with a splashy poke.

Umbrellas bloom like flowers bright,
As rafters sing throughout the night.
Each drop a note in nature's song,
A funny tune that can't go wrong.

So let's embrace the drip-drop beat,
With goofy steps and twinkling feet.
In sullen skies, we find delight,
With laughter flooding every night.

Soundscapes of the Slanted Showers

The showers fall at crazy angles,
Creating giggles like playful wrangles.
With every dribble on the ground,
A symphony of joy is found.

Sneaky splashes, quick surprise,
Make us leap with awkward highs.
Rain coats flapping, looking grand,
Too big, too small; it's a wet band.

Tap dancing ducks steal the show,
Skidding past in a slippery flow.
As puddle-jumpers take their turn,
We laugh aloud and twist and churn.

So let the drops fall where they may,
Creating whimsies in their play.
In slanted showers, fun will reign,
As we revel in our rainy gain.

Chords of the Chasing Clouds

Clouds are fluffy, like a cake,
Which makes me giggle, for goodness' sake.
With every pitter-patter beat,
The world transforms to a funny feat.

Umbrellas bloom like blooming flowers,
In colorful bursts, oh what powers!
As raindrops tap a silly tune,
We skip and twirl beneath the moon.

Singing songs of marshmallow days,
When skies play dress-up in magical ways.
Giggles ricochet with every splash,
An orchestra of fun, an epic clash.

So join the fun beneath the sky,
Where raindrops dance, and we can fly.
Chasing clouds and laughter too,
In this silly world made just for you.

Reflections of Rippling Rhythms

Drips like a leaky faucet, oh dear,
Get my umbrella, quick, my dear!
Puddles form a tiny sea,
Jumping in, just wait for me!

Rubber boots with colors bright,
Splashes made with pure delight.
Soaked from head to toe I stand,
Laughing hard, it's quite the band!

Clouds above look down and smirk,
It's a party, not some quirk.
Dancing raindrops tap my head,
In this shower, joy is spread!

Watch the worms do a jig, hey!
While I shuffle, sing, and play.
Nature's joke, it's such a sight,
Rainy days are pure delight!

Refrains from the Resplendent Rain

Pitter-patter, such a tune,
Making droplets dance by noon.
Umbrella cocktails on parade,
Watch those raindrops masquerade!

Cats and dogs scamper fast,
Hopping 'round like they're aghast.
But I've got my splashy shoes,
Who cares? I'll dance, I can't lose!

Rainbows peek through clouds of grey,
They giggle as the puddles play.
Flipping coins, I make a wish,
Splashing mud is my main dish!

Worms in tuxedos greet the storm,
Twisting, turning in their form.
Every drop a joyful cheer,
Silly fun, my friends are near!

The Poetry of Puddled Paths

Skippity hop from block to block,
Each puddle is a tick-tock clock.
With a splash, I write my verse,
Wiggly worms, oh how they disperse!

Raindrops race on rooftops high,
As squirrels glide, I wink and sigh.
Sidewalks gleam like glassy streams,
Where every step inspires dreams!

Let's hold a race, who'd win, tell me?
With rubber ducks on a tiny spree.
Posing for a soggy snap,
As water drips and drops, I clap.

Laughter echoes in the air,
Who knew puddles could bring such flair?
A splash of fun 'neath cloudy skies,
In this silly game, we rise!

Moistened Musings in Midsummer

Twirling raindrops on my nose,
Summer storms, as everyone knows.
Dancing like it's all okay,
Splashing through the clouds of gray!

Bouncing balls of water drop,
Hey look, they say, "Let's swap!"
I toss my hat, it takes a dive,
In this chaos, we all thrive!

Thunder rumbles, make a song,
Puddles sing where we belong.
With our fingers tracing lines,
Nature's quirkiness aligns!

Silly socks, oh what a sight,
Damp and joyful, oh what light!
As laughter lingers, dreams take flight,
In rainy whims, we find delight!

Verse of the Veiled Vistas

When droplets fall in jolly tones,
They skip and slide on window sills,
A tap-dancing troupe of tiny stones,
Each splash a giggle, each waltz fulfills.

The puddles laugh, they rippled wide,
With every jump from little feet,
A froggy crown, so spry with pride,
In nature's stage, the rain can't be beat!

Umbrellas twirl like disco balls,
As squishy shoes create a splash,
While thunder hums in giggly calls,
The stormy party? Quite the bash!

With every drop, the joy cascades,
A silly dance, a wet parade!

Balladry Beneath the Rainclouds

In the gloom, a snicker hides,
As woolly sheep skip down the lane,
With cotton candy, hearts collide,
Beneath the clouds, the laughter reigns.

Raindrops play tag on wrinkled coats,
A duck quacks 'bout a soggy fate,
He jumps in line with jumping goats,
An orchestra of wet and great!

The trees sway back to the tune,
Where breezes join the merry spree,
And puddles gleam like silver moons,
Oh joyous storm, you set us free!

Beneath the skies, the antics brew,
We dance and twirl, the world anew!

Allegretto of the Ambient Atmosphere

A soft serenade of drizzles plays,
With giggles soaring high and bold,
A melody that twirls and sways,
As dapper drops weave stories told.

When umbrellas meet in clumsy clash,
A smile exchanged in muddy haste,
While puddles pop with every splash,
A classic dance that won't be phased!

The raindrops trace their silly lines,
On noses twitching, faces bright,
In every drip, a joke combines,
To make the dullest day ignite!

In sync we'll hop from street to street,
Together in this rain-soaked beat!

Drizzle Dances and Daydreams

With rainy whispers, dreams take flight,
A world awash in tales so sweet,
Where raindrops jiggle with delight,
And laughter blooms beneath our feet.

In every splash, a chuckle grows,
As grumpy cats get drenched in glee,
They march around in soggy clothes,
Their shimmies spark a jubilee!

Dancing leaves and vibrant skies,
Invite the giddy hearts to sway,
With giggling friends, we improvise,
A stormy jamboree at play!

We twirl until the dusk is near,
With daydreams born from rainy cheer!

Serenade of the Storm

Pitter-patter prancing on my roof,
A troupe of raindrops with no sense of proof.
They slip and slide in a jolly dance,
While I sip my tea and watch their romance.

With every splash, they joke and cheer,
Making puddles that seem to leer.
They giggle as they splash on the street,
Wearing tiny boots on their little feet.

Umbrellas open in a parade so grand,
But they just giggle at the soggy land.
They splash me good in their playful spree,
Oh, to be a raindrop, wild and free.

When the skies clear, they wave goodbye,
Promising to return in a wink of an eye.
Collecting their laughter in drops to keep,
Until the next giggle begins a new leap.

Echoes Beneath the Clouds

Under clouds that brew a silly fuss,
Raindrops whisper, causing a rush.
They tickle rooftops with splashes true,
Making mischief in the bluest hue.

With each thud against the ground,
A family of jokes is often found.
They jump and bounce, oh what a sight,
Turning sidewalks into a slip-and-slide delight!

Splattered puddles reflect the skies,
Where tiny ducks wear comical ties.
They quack along with rhythmic glee,
In this cheerful, wet, wobbly spree.

As the rain bows down to take its bow,
Rascally drops dance, oh so how!
With a wink and a glance, they disappear,
Until next time, my watery dear!

Dancing Drops at Dusk

Evening falls, and the raindrops swirl,
Getting ready for a wobbly twirl.
They tango from the eaves, quite spry,
Playing hopscotch with the clouds up high.

They tip-toe lightly on windowpanes,
Drop by drop, like silly trains.
Each one lands with a bubbling laugh,
Making puddles as their autograph.

In their whirlwind, they find the fun,
Dressing up rooftops, one by one.
With a splash here, and a splat there,
They turn my lawn into a water fair!

Capping off the show with a finale bright,
They tip their hats as they take flight.
In a sudden breeze, they scatter and run,
Goodnight, sweet raindrops, you've had your fun.

Lullabies from the Sky

When the sky is restless, watch it rave,
Raindrops join in, their antics brave.
Tapping tunes on metal and glass,
Each patter echoes, a cheeky class.

Puddles form in a wiggly way,
While raindrops giggle and dance in play.
They swirl in circles, like kids at a fair,
Playing hopscotch and throwing clouds in the air.

They serenade me with a splashy beat,
Twirling around my dancing feet.
With a wink and nod, they fill the night,
In a bubbly chorus, oh what a sight!

As dreams take flight, the drops glisten bright,
Fading gently like stars in the night.
A final goodbye in a quirk and a dash,
Till tomorrow returns with another splash.

Chanting Clouds at Dawn

The clouds are singing, oh what a sound,
Their lyrics are funny as they float all around.
A tune of giggles, a rhythm of glee,
They dance in the sky with a cup of tea.

A fluffy ensemble, so plump and bright,
They joke with the sun, a comical sight.
"Psst, watch this move!" one cloud did declare,
As he tumbled and twisted, without a care.

Droplets fell down, like laughter from high,
Splashing the ground with a silly sigh.
The flowers were tickled, they shrieked in delight,
"Oh do it again, oh what a sight!"

So every dawn brings these antics anew,
Chanting clouds making life a fun view.
With laughter and joy, they float in a bunch,
Creating the perfect giggly brunch.

Drip Drops of Destiny

Drip drops are falling from the sky's embrace,
Each plop is a giggle, a wet little grace.
They travel on rooftops, with skittering glee,
A tap dance of fate, as funny as can be.

A raindrop once shouted, "I'm here to make waves!"
As puddles erupted, and ducks started raves.
"Join in the splash! Let's create a pool party!"
Said one little puddle, who's always so hearty.

The drain danced a jig, with a whirl and a spin,
"Catch me if you can!" made the raindrops grin.
They zigzagged and zoomed in a fabulous race,
While umbrellas chuckled, keeping up the pace.

In the midst of the fun, a drip took a dive,
"Can anyone tell me how to stay alive?"
To which all replied, with a cheer and a cheer,
"Just roll with the flow, and you'll conquer all fear!"

Beneath the Weeping Sky

Beneath the weeping sky, a scene so absurd,
The raindrops are laughing, not a word deferred.
Each droplet a comic, with stories to tell,
As they tumble and giggle, oh how they fell!

A raindrop once claimed, "I can tickle the breeze!"
As it splashed on a bird with the greatest of ease.
"Oh, stop it!" cried feather, "You're making me squeal!"
As he fluffed up his feathers, oh what a deal!

The sidewalks became stages for shows full of flair,
As puddles reflected the laughing affair.
A cacophony of chuckles filled the wet air,
With every drop falling, attention laid bare.

So here under showers, with giggles around,
We dance with the droplets, the joy that we've found.
A carnival of laughter, as we embrace the wet,
In a world where the skies give the best laughter yet!

Rhythms of the Resplendent Rain

Rhythms of downpour, such an upbeat show,
With raindrops tapping fast, just listen and go.
They play a sweet jig on the windowpanes,
A concert of chuckles that never restrains.

Each splat is a punchline, so heavy and light,
While gutters hum tunes, a musical sight.
"Let's form a band!" called a puddle named Ray,
As they jived and they swayed, all set for the play.

Neighbors peeked out, wearing hats of their own,
With hearts full of mirth, they joined in the tone.
The streets turned to stages for laughs on parade,
As the rhythms of rain made every joke played.

So dance in the downpour, embrace all the fun,
With every drippy drop, let the laughter run.
For life's a grand concert beneath skies so bright,
Where the rhythms of rain bring pure delight!

The Quotidian Quatrain of Quenching

When drops align and sing a tune,
Our hats become the big balloon.
A slip, a splash, we tip and teeter,
Is that a drink or just a litre?

The sky, a playful jester's cheer,
Drenches us without a fear.
Umbrellas float like jellyfish,
In puddles, dreams begin to swish.

As puddles grow, we leap and land,
Creating rivers, oh so grand.
We laugh aloud, our socks a mess,
Is this a curse or pure success?

At last, the sun peeks through the grey,
We dance like children, hip hooray!
In every drop, a story sprouted,
Who knew wet feet could leave us doubted!

Elegy in Every Erosion

A shower splatters on my head,
With squishy shoes, I fear I bled.
But wait! That was just muddy pie,
From dodging ducks that quack nearby.

Each drip, a giggle, swift and sly,
While raindrops dance and dip and fly.
Our clothes, a canvas of the storm,
As laughter makes the norm transform.

A misty window shows the scene,
Where rainbows peek through all the green.
Each drop that slips down on my chin,
Is just a tickle, let's begin!

So let the water, let it flow,
With every splash, our joy will grow.
An elegy for all that's wet,
Hilarious tales we won't forget!

Silhouettes against the Splash

In silhouettes, we dance at night,
With rain-soaked faces, what a sight!
Each hop creates a splash, a scene,
We're fishy friends in boots of green.

Raindrops play a trickster's game,
As laughter echoes, they're to blame.
We trip and slip, but who can frown,
When soggy socks are worn like crowns?

The world, a canvas wet and bright,
Reflecting joy in every light.
With each umbrella, flapping free,
We look like birds — just watch and see!

So let's embrace the drizzly fun,
While raindrops slide like tracks we run.
A splash of joy, a puddle's song,
With silly steps, we all belong!

Chasing Rainbows After Rain

A splash of color in the grey,
A rainbow's joke, in bright display.
We chase the hues with open hearts,
In puddles deep, the laughter starts.

Each step, a dance, a hopeful leap,
We splash through colors, wide and deep.
With giggles bright as sunlight's streak,
In wet socks, we become unique.

A painter's brush upon the ground,
Where watercolors swirl around.
We twirl and spin, our voices loud,
In every drop, we feel so proud.

So here we are, with joy unchained,
In every splash, fun is obtained.
Let's celebrate the happy game,
Of chasing rainbows, none the same!

Lyrical Lakes of the Heart

Puddles dance with daring leaps,
As rubber ducks launch from their heaps.
A frog in a tux, so bold and spry,
Hops around as raindrops fly.

GIS by the splash, a comic sight,
Umbrellas twist in a clumsy fight.
Squirrels in boots, they strut about,
Holding a meeting without a doubt.

Cowboy hats on puddles' heads,
Where drowning worms spin in their beds.
Singing songs on soft, damp ground,
Nobody knows what's lost and found.

Laughter echoes in the wet,
Chasing the sun, oh what a bet!
Join the waltz of water's whim,
In this bliss, we twirl and swim.

Whirls of Wet Wonder

A drip-drop dance from clouds so shy,
Kangaroos bounce as they say hi.
Raindrops fall like silly ducks,
Splashing giggles, gathering luck.

Wet socks squish in a jolly beat,
While giggling gremlins skip on their feet.
Colors spill from sloshing skies,
Painting smiles where laughter lies.

With each raindrop, tales unfold,
Of tiny trolls both brave and bold.
A jester spins, a water-spray,
Hopping through like it's a play.

In puddles deep, we take our plunge,
For rainy days are not for grunge.
Let's twirl about with joy and flair,
Under the drippy, glossy glare.

Whispers in the Drizzle

Whispers come from the dripping eaves,
As giggling kids don leafy sleeves.
A slippery slide made of pure fun,
Under a sky painted by the sun.

Silly cats with soggy tails,
Join in the game with giggling gales.
Worms twist in their wiggly jest,
In muddy puddles, they find their rest.

Chickens dance a feathery reel,
Flapping wildly—a comical deal.
The dripping roofs chant their sweet tune,
As frogs debate what's best to croon.

Forget your woes, let laughter reign,
In this bosom of water and rain.
We'll whistle and hum as clouds conspire,
To fill our hearts with joyous fire.

Melodies of the Monsoon

Thunder rumbles in a playful tease,
While raindrops shimmy through the trees.
Dancing slippers splash in brown,
As quirky clouds play dress-up clown.

A sloth with style slips on the street,
Sliding and gliding on tiny feet.
The weather sings a wacky song,
We clap along, right or wrong!

Birds with hats dodge the rain,
Sipping tea in a lovely lane.
Umbrellas bloom like flowers wide,
Colorful bursts in a water slide.

As puddles giggle and stones sigh,
Clouds puff up and wave goodbye.
We chase the sun with heart so light,
In the sprinkle-dazzle, life feels bright.

Odes from Overcast Skies

A droplet danced upon my nose,
It tickled funny, like a rose.
With every splash, a fleeting thrill,
The clouds conspire, they laugh at will.

Puddles grow, a sneaky game,
My shoes are drenched, but who's to blame?
The skies are gray, yet laughter's bright,
As raindrops play their merry flight.

Umbrellas flip, a circus act,
They fly away, and that's a fact.
The raindrops giggle, fall and tease,
While I just slip, oh what a breeze!

So come, my friend, let's jump and splash,
In watery worlds where time can dash.
With every drop, a chuckling sound,
In overcast joy, we're all spellbound.

Cadence of the Cloudburst

A storm approached with pitter-pats,
And frogs croaked out in silly chats.
Where puddles formed, my dog took flight,
His leaps were comical, pure delight.

A little bird in rain gear sleek,
Sipped raindrops like a can of peek.
He fluffed his feathers, looked so grand,
Might start a band, there on the sand.

The umbrella's up, but twirls it does,
Like a dancer, finding what it was.
With every gust, it spins around,
And twirls me off the soaking ground.

The rain's a jester, full of glee,
While clowns of thunder dance with me.
In this delight, let voices cheer,
In cloudburst fun, we'll shed a tear.

Tones of the Tumbling Drops

A tap, a rap, a soft little sound,
The raindrops fall, they leap and bound.
Each drop a giggle, a tiny jest,
Oh what a prank, oh what a test!

I try to catch one on my tongue,
But slippery tricks have just begun.
They splash my face, they fly on by,
It's laughter's fault, oh my oh my!

The grass is slick, I lose my stand,
With every slip, it's quite unplanned.
But giggles rise, from clouds above,
In every splash, it's joy I love.

So let us dance beneath the skies,
Where droplets fall and laughter flies.
In this parade of water's play,
We'll laugh together, day after day.

Cadences in the Cleansed Air

The puddles shine like smiling eyes,
Reflecting clouds in goofy guise.
The sun peeks out, a prankster's game,
In this wet world, we cheer his name.

Raindrops play hopscotch on the ground,
While giggles form in every sound.
They bounce and break in playful cheer,
Making sure the fun is near.

I saw a cat with soggy paws,
A funny sight that gave me pause.
She shook her fur, a soggy show,
And danced about, not wanting to go.

So as we whirl in joyful glee,
The rain may fall, but we're so free.
Let laughter lead in every splash,
In cleansed air, our spirits clash.

Tuning Forks of the Tempest

When clouds begin to laugh and play,
A symphony of drops on a sunny day.
Umbrellas dance like they've lost their mind,
While puddles giggle, leaving worries behind.

The wind joins in with a playful shout,
Telling rainy tales, there's never a doubt.
A splash here and there, it's all quite absurd,
As frogs serenade with a croaky word.

Kids leap and twirl in the watery cheer,
While ducks form a band, spreading joy far and near.
Each splash is a note in this melody glee,
A fun-filled performance, just wait and see!

The lightning strikes a pose, takes a bow,
While thunder rolls in, "Did you catch that now?"
Nature's own circus, we laugh all the same,
Under the rain, let's all play this game!

Echoing Drops at Dusk

As twilight whispers a gentle tune,
Raindrops dribble down, a bubbly cartoon.
Each drop is a giggle, a chuckle, a cheer,
Bouncing off rooftops, oh, what a dear!

Puddles gather round, like fans at a show,
Watching the droplets dance soft and slow.
They jump to the rhythm, each plop seems to play,
A joke in the storm, don't let it slip away!

With ducks in tuxedo, they waddle and glide,
While frogs crack up, their buoyant pride.
The giggling sky, it showers confetti,
Making us laugh, is it really too petty?

As shadows stretch long and raindrops conclude,
We reminisce over the fun and the mood.
Echoing drops, oh, the laughter they bring,
Under the dusk, let our chuckles take wing!

Songs of Soothing Showers

In showers of giggles, the droplets arrive,
Tickling our noses, bringing us alive.
Each splash sings a tune of the silliest kind,
While clouds in their petticoats twirl and unwind.

The rooftops hum softly, a tap dance parade,
Creating a melody that never will fade.
Bubbles of laughter float high to the moon,
As raindrops conspire to play a sweet tune.

Jumping through puddles like bouncing balloons,
Sprinkling the world with delightful cartoons.
A storm of laughter, let the fun not cease,
Nature's own jesters, bringing us peace.

So let's tip our hats to the soaking embrace,
Where joy is the music in this wild chase.
As skies draw their curtains on whirlwinds of cheer,
We'll cherish the symphony, year after year!

Syllables in the Sleet

Sleet sings softly, a curious sound,
Whispering secrets as it tumbles around.
Each drop is a giggle, a playful jest,
Mischief in nature, never at rest.

Icicles hang like a frozen grin,
While snowmen waddle, they're ready to spin.
Frost bites our noses, but we don't complain,
With laughter as armor against winter's reign.

Paddle-boats float on a sleety sea,
But ducks wear their sunglasses, how funny to see!
As winter recites in its chilly ballet,
We'll dance in the laughter, come what may.

With snowflakes like confetti, we shake off the chill,
Every flurry of fun, a heart to fulfill.
So let's toast to the sleet, like a cocktail of cheer,
In this winter wonderland, we'll keep laughter near!

Whispers of Water's Dance

Pitter-patter on the roof,
The raindrops are in quite a goof.
They dance around in playful spry,
As if the clouds are asking, 'Why?'

Silly puddles start to jig,
With each drop, they leap and dig.
They splash and flop with muddy cheer,
Chasing frogs, the croak is clear!

Umbrellas spin like rooftops fly,
While squirrels pop like popcorn, oh my!
They slip and slide in slick parade,
Each little misstep a grand charade.

So when the storms roll through your town,
Remember laughter wears a crown.
Nature's antics bring delight,
In water's playful, funny flight.

Melodies in the Mist

Misty mornings have a tune,
Where dew drops dance beneath the moon.
They giggle softly on the grass,
As raindrops tumble, none can pass.

Every leaf begins to sway,
In rhythm with the water's play.
They sway and twirl in damp delight,
As tiny bugs prepare for flight.

The wind joins in with a silly blow,
Sending raindrops to and fro.
A serenade of drips and drops,
As the laughter never stops.

So if you hear that light refrain,
Just know it's joking with the rain.
Nature's music so absurd,
With every splash, a giggle stirred.

Serenade of the Storm

The thunder claps like it's a show,
While raindrops laugh and dance below.
Lightning winks, a cheeky tease,
As wet squirrels shimmy in the breeze.

Puddles form like laughing pools,
Jumping kids break all the rules.
They splash and squeal, no care of shoe,
In this stormy hullabaloo!

Clouds juggle raindrops, what a sight,
As umbrellas turn into flight.
They twirl and spin, then topple down,
Wearing the most ridiculous frown.

So when storms come with grins so wide,
Join in the revelry, take a ride.
Feel the joy, it's boundless glee,
In this silly, soggy jubilee!

Echoes Beneath the Clouds

Underneath those heavy shrouds,
The world erupts in laughter loud.
Raindrops drip like jokes long told,
With every splash, new stories unfold.

The fleeting rainbows stretch and bow,
Saying, "Look at us! We're wow!"
They tease the sun to peek a clue,
While slippery worms join in the brew.

The wind whistles with a scoff,
As branches wave and leaves fall off.
Oh what fun, the critters cheer,
With every murmur of the sphere.

So let the drops fall where they may,
In puddles deep or on the hay.
For every chuckle from above,
Brings forth a joy that we all love.

Poems from the Pattering Sky

Raindrops dance on my roof like mice,
While I count their twirls, oh isn't that nice?
They tumble and splash with giggles galore,
Making me laugh till my cheeks start to sore.

Puddles form stories, a slippery path,
I slip and I slide, what a slippery math!
A puddle whispers, 'Come take a glance,'
But it laughs harder when I lose my stance.

Clouds wear a hat that's a little too bright,
Feeling so groovy, they dance through the night.
I swear they chuckle, do you hear that sound?
As I jump in the puddles, their joy knows no bound.

So here's to the rain with its playful delight,
It splashes our giggles and blankets the night.
Next time it falls, we'll invite it to play,
With hearts full of laughter, we'll splosh on our way.

Verses on Vibrant Puddles

Puddles around me like mirrors of fun,
Reflecting my dance in the warmth of the sun.
I splash and I laugh like a quirky old fool,
Who found a new joy in an everyday pool.

With each little drop falls another big smile,
My sneakers are drenched, but it's totally worthwhile.
Jumping in puddles, my soggy parade,
The water applauds - what a splashing charade!

When raindrops compete for the title of best,
I blow them a kiss, they'll never rest!
"The more the merrier," I'm sure they all say,
As I twirl in my raincoat and dance down the gray.

So here's to the puddles, bright mirrors of cheer,
I dive into laughter; there's nothing to fear.
With splashes and giggles, together we'll play,
Thank you, dear clouds, for this whimsical display!

Lyrics of the Looming Light

Gray clouds loom over, but I'm ready to cheer,
With my gumboots on, I have nothing to fear.
I smile up at the sky, they dribble and drip,
While I dance like a jelly, with a wobbly hip.

The sun peeks through cracks with a glint in its eye,
"Oh look, here comes water!" I hear it all sigh.
They're ready to party; it's time to unite,
With raindrops so funny, they lighten the night.

Little droplets tumble, all jiggly and spry,
They play tag on my head, I'll never deny.
The thunder's a DJ, his beats loud and clear,
As it booms, the raindrops just dance without fear.

So let's gather together, all joyful and bright,
In this wacky concert, we'll groove out of sight.
With shimmering puddles and clouds up above,
We'll laugh till we drop; it's a rainstorm of love!

Ballads Beneath the Thunder

Thunder rolls in with a skip and a hop,
Makes me think twice before I take a drop.
But with every big boom, I chuckle and grin,
For rain's just a party I'm ready to win.

The raindrops come down with a playful intent,
As I jump and I splash in sheer merriment.
The clouds have a riot, they rumble with glee,
Turning my street into a laughing spree.

Kicking up water, it's a slippery show,
As my friends gather 'round, we all want to go.
To dance in the rain, with squeals and delight,
While the thunder hums tunes, warming up the night.

So here's to the storms and the ways they amuse,
In each drop, a giggle, in each laugh, a muse.
Nothing beats laughter when skies turn so gray,
Let's dance in the rain, make it a bright day!

Chants of the Cascading Clouds

Droplets dancing on my head,
They giggle as I jump from bed.
An umbrella flipped, a sight so grand,
A battle lost to the windy hand.

Puddles laughing, making a splash,
Wearing gumboots, I make a dash.
With every trip, there's a fun little fall,
Chants of laughter echo through it all.

Raindrops tickle my nose and chin,
The silly sounds make me grin.
A rooftop symphony, what a show,
I dance along as they come and go.

Clouds parade in a soaked-up spree,
As nature sings, I feel so free.
Each splash and plop, a playful tease,
Cascading chaos—a joy to seize.

Verses in the Vapor

The clouds are moody, don't you see?
Hiding sunshine, just for glee.
They sprinkle down as if to say,
'Let's make the world a wet ballet!'

Dancing raindrops, where did they go?
Peeking from corners, putting on a show.
Squirrels skitter, dodging the drops,
While I stomp loudly—splash, splat, plops!

Kites take cover, with a frown and pout,
But oh, the fun! Just hear me shout.
Races with rivers, rolling with cheer,
Each puddle's a party, oh my dear!

In drizzle's embrace, we all unite,
With laughter and joy, oh, what a sight!
So let it rain, let it fall true,
In verses of vapor, it's all brand new.

Songs of the Soggy Streets

Wet shoes squeak as I zig and zag,
Muddy splashes, oops, what a brag!
The sidewalks shimmer like they dance,
Each step I take, another chance.

Bicycles wobble as wheels go round,
Chasing rainbows when puddles are found.
Rubber duckies leap from the car,
Floating along—oh, how bizarre!

Raindrops racing, what's the score?
I cheer them on, then trip—oh no more!
But then I laugh, I'm not alone,
The soggy streets are our wet-zone.

And when it's over, the sun peeks through,
Just wait, I'm back to my giggling crew.
With sunlight's kiss, we twirl and sway,
Songs of the soggy, hip-hip-hooray!

The Poetry of Pitter-Patter

Pitter-patter, here comes the show,
A parade of droplets, row by row.
Each one whispers secrets of fun,
While I chase shadows, oh, what a run!

I twirl with raindrops, what a delight,
Ducking and diving, oh, what a sight!
A friendly storm just can't be tamed,
With giggles and glee, I feel so famed.

The skies blush pink as they play their part,
While I splash puddles straight from the heart.
Clouds whisper jokes that I can't ignore,
Each giggle and chuckle just opens a door.

And when it ends, what do I see?
A rainbow smiles back at me.
So bring the thunder, let the skies collide,
In poetry's embrace, let laughter abide.

Windsongs and Wet Leaves

Puddles dance in silly shoes,
As raindrops play a game of blues.
Squirrels slip, then start to slide,
Chasing their tails, oh what a ride!

Umbrellas flip like little boats,
While water drips from soggy coats.
A duck quacks jokes from the wet street,
As kids rush to dodge his webbed feet!

Raincoats shimmer, colors bright,
Splashing friends with sheer delight.
Laughter echoes, spirits soar,
Covered in mud, we all want more!

So let it pour, let it flow,
We'll splash in puddles, row by row.
With windsongs singing through the trees,
We'll dance with joy, as light as breeze!

Lyrics in the Liquid Light

Rain taps lightly on the roof,
A musical beat that brings the goof.
Wind chimes rattle a merry tune,
While frogs croak jokes beneath the moon.

Dancing droplets join the jive,
Chasing flowers that come alive.
With each puddle, a mirror shines,
Reflecting mischief in playful lines.

A slippery slide down every path,
We laugh till we're soaked, feel the aftermath.
Giggling, puddling, what a sight,
'Cause every splash is pure delight!

Come join the fun, don't stay dry,
With muddy shoes, we'll leap and fly.
Together we'll sing through the stormy fright,
In the joyful chaos of liquid light!

Narratives of the Glistening Ground

Each raindrop tells a funny tale,
Of goofy clouds that start to sail.
Mushrooms pop, they're here to boast,
The wettest party, let's raise a toast!

Ants march proudly, one by one,
Raindance practice, isn't it fun?
They slip and slide, then stand up tall,
In their tiny world, they have a ball!

The puddles reflect our silly grins,
With splashes made, our laughter spins.
Little feet stomp, a joyful sound,
Crafting legends from the glistening ground.

Jokes in the rain, wild and free,
Every drop a chance to be goofy.
Let's skip along, make memories bright,
With splashy stories, pure delight!

Epistles from the Eclipsed Sun

Though clouds loom overhead in grey,
We send our laughter out to play.
With each raindrop that plops down,
We write our notes in pure clown town!

Ducks wear hats, and frogs wear shoes,
Each letter drips with playful news.
We scribble tales on grass so green,
While in the chaos, we reign supreme!

From muddy skies to fields of fun,
We'll keep laughing till the day is done.
So let the sun hide, let shadows run,
For joy blooms bright, eclipsing none!

With every splash, a giggle pops,
As rain keeps rolling, the laughter hops.
We send this message through the rain:
Let's dance, let's sing, let's cheer again!

www.ingramcontent.com/pod-product-compliance
Lightning Source LLC
Chambersburg PA
CBHW071844160426
43209CB00003B/404